# FRAGMENTS

By the same author
*Abandoned: A Life of Shadows.*

# FRAGMENTS

## Echo of the Past

KATE TAYLOR

Cover photo © Mihai Tamasila
Illustration © *Young Sad Woman* By Diless

National Library of New Zealand Cataloguing-in-Publication Data

Taylor, Kate
Fragments : echo of the past / Kate Taylor
ISBN 978-0-473-25332-5
I. Title.
NZ821.3—dc 23

# INTRODUCTION

These fragments of thought show why being told to wear bright colours, take up sport and laugh more, are a ridiculous and redundant approach to depression. A broken or lost soul needs to be listened to, not talked at.

During my long and difficult journey, I have found a good doctor, good friends, loving cats, therapy, medication and an outlet for self expression to be the most beneficial tools for an improved authentic life.

Do not aim to be the best person you think you should be, or the person you used to be, be the best person you are today and take life one day at time.

To Be or not to Be.

My mind feels fractured

A kaleidoscope of fragments

From inside the looking glass

A web of lies looks back.

Do you think

You could ever find

The answer to the Universe

Inside your mind


Do you think

You could ever see

The beauty of the Universe

Inside of me?

Freedom —

A perception in mind

And the prisoner weeps.

Dying —

Sacrificing yourself

To please others.

You hand me a tissue

To wipe away my tears


Pity you didn't care enough

To stop them in the first place


How can you see the effect

But distance yourself from the cause?

Why would you

        want me to be

Such a shadow

        of who I really am?

You don't see me


You look at my actions

And draft an image

That is irrelevant.

Cold    hard    and    indifferent

You    wade    through    my    pain

With            such            contempt

Because    it's    more    alive

Than you'll ever be

And you see it.

Death — The ultimate in hiding.

True loneliness

Is a broken person

With baggage

Speaking a language

No-one can understand.

Little pieces of me fly away

As time marches on


Lack of respect for the Self

Lacking respect for self


Trapped within.

Words achingly drip

From my wounded lips

Time seals shut the door

On my pain

On my life

I am no more

I feel no more

I am not.

What is the point

Of meeting with you

When you act

Like I'm not

There anyway

Acting like puppets

On a stage

From an ancient

Unchanging script

Time and time again.

It's hard to respect yourself

When no one else does.

You resent my freedom

You deny my individuality

You dismiss my pain

And laugh at my struggle.

Pain really is a solo journey.

Year after year

Time after time

Tear after tear


An unexpressed life

Mourns to be freed.

A tolling bell echoes in my head

Another dream falls down dead


Tears

Stream

Down

My face


A world of purpose


                    Me out of place.

Blood spills

From raked flesh


The air

Is pungent with decay


A tortured soul

Laments its existence.

Alone

I hear my footsteps echo

I hear my heart break

I see my dreams die

And I know you are smiling

At my pain and yet strangely

You can't understand

My anger and hatred for you.

The best friends

Give you the freedom

To be yourself

Even if it's at the expense

Of that friendship.

There is no hope here

Only death

And it hurts to die

Slowly

Endlessly

Where is hope now?

Time covers pain

Until we forget

The feeling

Of being born

To an ugly world

Bent on decay

Decomposing minds

And this we call life


To die is to be born

Freedom at birth.

Unfelt thoughts echo

Uneasy feelings arise


A life in crisis.

It's too deep for words

This vast

Empty

Aching void

That's always present.

Through shattered dreams

And frozen tears

I held on to the thought of you

The romanticised ideal salvation

Hoping you would rescue me

From my life

And envelop me in yours.

Memories peeled back

To reveal truth

Relived with aching intensity

Moments frozen in time

Fossils trapped in mind.

Truth is the way and the goal

It is beyond good and evil

It exists

Therefore it Is

It is also subjective

Relative to our experiences

Freedom at the point of application.

You stop to ask

How I am today

I reply I'm fine


To your back as you walk away.

I am the pain

That never fades

The constant ache

Remnants of the past

Too vast to comprehend.

There is no humour here

I am stripped bare

All pretence fallen away

Wounds too deep to heal

Refusing their camouflage.

My hands are bloodied and torn

From desperately crawling

Over the remnants

Of a shattered existence

In a vain attempt for freedom.

Now I have stopped running

There is nowhere left to hide

I am drowning in black

Surrounded by living shadows

Full of haunting echoes —

The nightmares of the past

That live on in the waking world

Condemning me to relive them again.

My tears flow feely

As former days are recalled

From the storage of memory

The home of living wounds

Where unexpected sources

Trigger the release

Of long forgotten incidents

To be intensely relived again.

Tears of ink freely flowing

Adhering to its own rhythm

To capture pain

And transform it into a form

That you can understand.

# ABOUT THE AUTHOR

Kate Taylor was born in Auckland, New Zealand, where she continues to reside. She lives with her rescued fluffy feline princess, Abby and enjoys watching her swing on the curtains, chase flies and chew on all her cardboard boxes.